KITCHENS

KITCHENS

Exciting Ideas for Creating the Kitchen You've Always Wanted

John Driemen

HPBooks

HPBooks, Inc.
P.O. Box 5367
Tucson, AZ 85703
(602) 888-2150

Publisher: Rick Bailey
Executive Editor: Randy Summerlin

ISBN: 0-89586-501-7 (hardcover)
0-89586-525-4 (paperback)

Library of Congress Catalog Card Number: 86-82118

KITCHENS: Exciting Ideas for Creating the Kitchen You've Always Wanted
was prepared and produced by
Quarto Marketing Ltd.
15 West 26th Street
New York, NY 10010

Editor: Pamela Hoenig
Art Director: Mary Moriarty
Designer: Liz Trovato
Photo Editor: Susan M. Duane
Photo Research: Sherry Gilligan
Production Manager: Karen L. Greenberg

Typeset by B.P.E. Graphics
Color separations by South Seas Graphic Art Company
Printed and bound in Hong Kong by Leefung-Asco Printers Ltd.

Acknowledgments

Two people deserve to be thanked for
contributions they have made toward the writing of this book:
Lloyd Jafvert, a fine residential architect, counselor
and friend gave me a verbal encyclopedia
of classic "before" kitchens he had been commissioned to remodel
during his 20 years of professional practice, and then
patiently helped me organize it all into the
diagnostic list included in Chapter 2.
And Robert Hoffman, workshop editor
and former colleague at Home Mechanix, for sharing his how-to expertise
on the spice rack presented in Chapter 5.

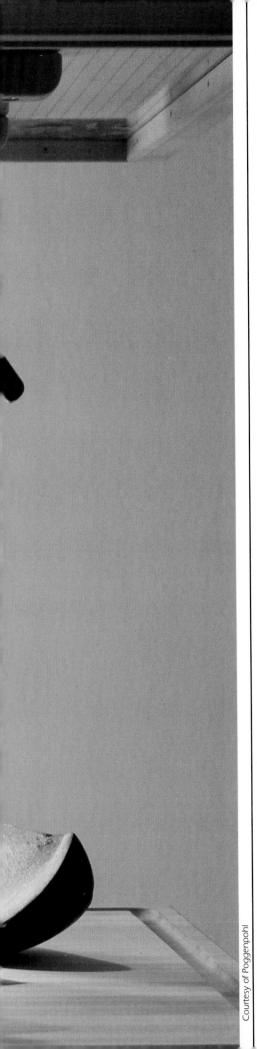

CONTENTS

Introduction

Photo: Daniel Eifert; Design: Larry Bogdanow

Introduction

 o question about it, the kitchen is the most popular room in the house. Most of us never clock the amount of time we spend in our kitchens, but if we did, it would add up to an astonishing 50 percent of our at-home time.

Stop and think about it. Besides three meals a day, there are between-meal snacks—after school for the kids and late night for ourselves. Then there's baking for holidays and special occasions, along with canning and freezing in the fall. During the summer, the kitchen is the base of operations for outdoor cooking and lawn and garden work. It's the always-available refreshment stand on hot afternoons.

Throughout the year, the kitchen serves us in ways we seldom think of: It's where we make shopping lists, clip coupons, pay bills, use the phone to attend to daily household business and enjoy a quiet cup of coffee with friends who drop by.

Entertaining is another good workout for the kitchen. Not only should the kitchen rise to the occasion and function perfectly when the job is cooking dinner for 20, but it also should provide a comfortable space for people to congregate. You may drink in the living room and eat in the dining room, but the real life of the party is usually in the kitchen. Its natural informality draws guests like a magnet.

Because you use your kitchen constantly, it's important that the design and decor feel comfortable to you, reflecting your personal sense of style. But first it must be a functional room, a place where day-in and day-out cooking tasks can be handled efficiently and pleasantly. Your kitchen must naturally complement your skills as a homemaker just as a woodworking shop complements the skills of a craftsman. If it doesn't work this way, then it doesn't work very well.

Looking at your kitchen from the perspective of your checkbook, it represents a considerable portion of your home's worth. Yet in spite of the substantial price tag, kitchen remodeling is the most popular large-scale home fix-up project with roughly $17.8 billion retail spent annually. And while the luxury kitchen redos may not add more than their exact dollar cost to the value of the house, statistics confirm that this is usually money well spent. Figures kept by both the National Kitchen and Bath Association and the American Association of Realtors reveal that for every dollar you invest in kitchen remodeling within the range of $2,500 to $10,000, $4 will come back when you sell the house.

A well-designed kitchen, then, makes good sense. But converting the chaos of your existing kitchen into a stylish, multifunction room can seem like a journey fraught with dead ends and wrong turns. The range of kitchen products, from appliances to tiles to cabinets, is so vast and ever changing that it seems impossible for the one-time remodeler to make intelligent choices without professional help. Understanding those choices and getting the appropriate, qualified help is what this book is about.

Photo: John Driemen; Stylist: Patricia Carpenter

CHAPTER 1

Concept and Style

Photo: Norman McGrath; Design: Michael Rubin

Clean lines and a no-nonsense, industrial look characterize today's high-tech kitchen. Here, two sinks provide clean-up convenience and the center points for two separate work areas. A large vent hood easily handles the two cooktops, and multireceptacle plug molds, which are built into the hood's frame, provide electricity for kitchen accessories.

J. Michael Kanouff

Contrasting with the clean high-tech look (opposite page) is the classic design of this efficient country-style kitchen. A decorative semicircular window spans across four 8-light casement windows, giving the room the feel of an English country gazebo. To take advantage of the light and the view, both cooktop and sink are set beneath the windows.

Kitchen style and decor is mainly a matter of personal taste. A well-designed country kitchen will perform its job the same as an equally well-designed high-tech kitchen. For most people, style is predetermined by what already exists in the rest of the house, or in the rooms adjacent to the kitchen. Unless the kitchen remodeling is part of an extensive addition that includes other living spaces, such as a family room, few homeowners stray far from the existing style of the house.

More to the point is deciding what kitchen layout—U-shaped, peninsular or island—best suits the space available and whether or not to include an eating area as part of the kitchen plan.

In this chapter, we'll look at ways to make this choice and also analyze kitchens of many styles to see why and how they work.

Richard S. Mandelkorn

Above: When space is at a premium, consider creating a work counter that also doubles as a sit-down eating bar.

Courtesy of Quakermaid

Corners are dead spots in many kitchens. In this space-restricted kitchen, a combination range and microwave oven, placed in the corner, allows more counter to be used as work surface.

Photo: Durston Saylor, Design: Shope, Reno and Wharton

Skylights are an effective way to add light to any room and are especially appropriate in a kitchen where good lighting is part of good design. Here, glass-door cabinets harmonize perfectly with the skylights above.

Photo: Lea Babcock; Design: Mary Jane Pappas

With so many household activities centered in the kitchen, building a place for working on noncooking tasks is a plus. Sometimes called a kitchen planning center, the area includes a desk, open storage for books and papers and drawers that double as filing cabinets.

J. Michael Kanouff

A custom-made, copper vent hood combines function with design in this Spanish-style kitchen island. Ceramic tile, an ideal material for setting down hot pots, is easy to clean and scorch-resistant.

J. Michael Kanouff

Courtesy of Bosch

Using a kitchen skylight to create an atrium, as shown here, is an ingenious idea. When skylights are employed as the sole or principal source of natural light, make certain that at least one of them opens to provide ventilation.

Left and below: While the principles of good kitchen design mandate efficiently placed appliances, anything goes when it comes to decorating. The odds and ends that give this kitchen its charm, including a fully restored antique range, testify to years of collecting by the owner.

J. Michael Kanouff

Richard S. Mandelkorn

Above: When planning an eat-in kitchen or a kitchen-family room combination, consider adding a fireplace. If your house has an existing chimney flue, you may be able to use it, providing your installation meets local building codes. Otherwise, you can install an insulated metal chimney stack, an alternative that gives greater latitude in positioning the new fireplace.

Facing page: Laminates give a kitchen its glitter. Three major laminate manufacturers, Formica, Nevermar and Wilsonart, provide an almost unlimited palette of colors and patterns from which to choose.

Courtesy of Millbrook Custom Kitchens

Steel trusses, part of this modern loft renovation, set the style for the kitchen. In many lofts the kitchen, built into a single wall, also serves to divide the loft. When this happens, the major appliances are usually lined up along the same wall, resulting in diminished kitchen efficiency.

Courtesy of Moben Kitchens

Courtesy of Poggenpohl

Many European cabinets make no attempt to hide pots and pans behind closed doors. These sleek, pull-out metal shelves are an integral element in a stripped-down, functional design scheme.

Apartment living has a definite impact on kitchen design. When space is tight, innovation and improvisation are the keys to a successful layout. Here, a freestanding unit serves as a room divider, provides a small table for eating and offers both storage space and countertop work area.

CHAPTER 2
Planning

Finding Out What's Wrong

Careful planning is step one for any kitchen remodeling project. The time and effort spent here will be repaid handsomely with a kitchen that reflects your lifestyle, meets your needs and has the built-in flexibility to accommodate new needs as they arise. Good planning includes judicious financial planning and means keeping a critical eye on costs so the kitchen you plan will be the kitchen you can afford.

Chances are your present kitchen suffers from "terminal inefficiency," and the best thing you can say about it is that it's charming—as long as you don't have to cook in it. Start your planning phase by listing all those things you don't like about it.

The barometer for measuring a kitchen's efficiency is called the *work triangle.* To understand how the work triangle works, make a quick sketch of your present kitchen, noting the location of the refrigerator, range and sink. These appliances represent the three work centers every kitchen must have: a place for storage and preparation (the refrigerator), a cooking center (the range) and a cleanup area (the sink). Now connect these points to form a triangle. Your kitchen's efficiency is measured in the steps you have to take between these work centers. The most efficient kitchen

Photo: John Driemen; Stylist: Patricia Carpenter

Above: **Except for creating an efficient kitchen work triangle, there are no hard and fast rules for developing a good design. Here, the family lifestyle suggests a single, circular work space as the kitchen focal point. The multipurpose counter allows several people to work together and make use of the countertop appliances conveniently stored behind tambour doors. A circular fluorescent fixture picks up the work-space design while providing sufficient general illumination for the entire kitchen.**

Facing page: **Open storage for dishes and glassware has created something of a controversy among kitchen designers. The pros are that you know where everything is and are not restricted when you want to reach for something. The cons are that items left in the open collect dust and are more likely to fall and break if handled carelessly.**

layouts are those in which the total distance between the work centers adds up to no more than 22 feet and no less than 12 feet. And if your sink, range and refrigerator don't form a triangle at all, you can bet that you often find yourself tripping over your own feet during meal preparation. Put a tape measure to your own kitchen and see how it measures up.

Here's a checklist for finding other kitchen trouble spots:

Countertops

• Is there a place to put down bags of groceries when you come home from a shopping trip?

• Do you have counter space next to the range or cooktop for setting down hot pans?

• If you have a wall oven, is there space nearby to set down food coming out of the oven?

• Is there enough counter space next to the sink to stack dirty dishes?

• Is there space on the other side of the sink for a dish drainer?

• Do your counters have back-splashes?

Storage

• Do you have to store food in hard-to-reach cabinets above the refrigerator, oven or cooktop?

• Do you have difficulty finding things in corner cabinets?

• Is there a place to store raw vegetables near the sink?

• Is there a lot of wasted space on shelves because spice jars have to coexist with cereal boxes?

• Can you keep your dishes near your dishwasher?

• Is there convenient and safe storage space near the sink for household chemicals?

Ventilation

• Do you have at least one window that can be opened?

• Is there an exhaust fan or vent hood above the range or cooktop?

Lighting

• Does your kitchen have a ceiling light?

• Can you use 150-watt bulbs in it?

• Is there a light fixture above the sink?

• Is there enough light on work counters to see the food you're preparing?

Miscellaneous

• Do your appliances belong in a museum?

• Is dirt a permanent part of your walls?

Courtesy of SieMatic

Choosing A Design That Works

Start planning your new kitchen by taking measurements of your old one. Do this as accurately as possible, noting the exact locations of windows, doors, closets, stairways and other components. Use these measurements to make a plan on graph paper.

Professional kitchen designers draw plans using a scale in which ½ inch equals 1 foot; you should do the same. If you're using ¼-inch graph paper, this means that each square will equal 6 inches. When noting dimensions on your plan, mark them in inches rather than feet, because kitchen cabinets are measured in inches. This will save you from having to convert your measurements later on when you order new cabinets. For reference, measure any adjoining room that you might consider expanding into and mark those dimensions on the graph paper also.

Experiment with various designs by laying tracing paper over your graph-paper plan and sketching new layouts. Keep the principles of the work triangle in mind, using the graph paper to keep the legs of the triangle within accepted length.

Concurrent with your sketching, make a list of everything you would like to include in your new kitchen. This is your wish list. If you

Photo: Daniel Eifert; Design: Linda Langsam

Above: Sometimes a single lighting scheme can provide both general illumination and task lighting. Here, decorative fixtures capable of taking 75-watt bulbs provide good overall lighting and can also be directed to throw light onto key work areas. The light track is long enough to accommodate additional fixtures, should they be required.

Facing page: Increasingly, cooktops include efficient exhaust vents. This eliminates installing a ceiling mounted vent when the cooktop is part of a work island. When not in use, this vent retracts into the cooktop, as pictured in the photograph.

decide to get professional design help, the list and your preliminary sketches will give the designer a good idea of what you want.

Design Professionals

There are four major sources for kitchen design help: architects, certified kitchen designers, remodeling contractors and kitchen showrooms.

If your new kitchen is part of a larger remodeling project that involves an addition to your house or a major rearrangement of rooms, you should opt for an architect. They have the engineering knowledge needed to deal with the structural problems that occur when an addition is built onto an older house. Architects normally charge 8 to 15 percent of the total building cost, although if you want only design consultation and you don't need a full set of structural plans, the fee will be considerably lower.

A certified kitchen designer is a professional approved by the National Kitchen and Bath Association. Because these designers are specialists, they are usually more familiar with current trends in kitchen design and new products. Fees will probably be lower than those you would pay an architect, but expect to part with at least $1,000 for the preliminary design work. At your request, certified kitchen designers can also produce working drawings for a contractor or act as the contractor themselves.

If you choose a remodeling contractor, make sure that he or she is a specialist in kitchens and ask to see examples of previous work. This is a good idea for architects and certified kitchen designers also, although the latter are likely to have a portfolio of photographed work for your inspection and will probably insist that you look at it before you sign any agreement.

Kitchen showrooms exist to sell and install cabinets and accessory items. They may represent a manufacturer, or the company may do custom work. In both cases, their first interest is selling a product, so they are less likely to have the design expertise offered by architects and designers. Whatever design services they do offer, however, will be free, because the cost is built into the cabinet price.

Budgeting Your Kitchen Remodel

Unfortunately, the sky is the limit when it comes to pricing a kitchen remodel. You can pay more for imported cabinets than it would cost to build a new house in many parts of the country. Floor tile sells anywhere from $2 to $15 per square foot. However, if your taste runs to imported, hand-painted tiles, expect to pay as much as $20 for an individual tile. Laminates for counter tops range between $1.10 and $4.50 a square foot. The list of computer-controlled appliances and labor-saving gadgets that you can buy is endless. Labor costs for remodeling are high, reaching $200 per square foot.

J. Michael Kanouff

Computer-Aided Design

It should come as no surprise that computers have entered the field of kitchen design. Some home-center stores and large retailers of home-oriented products now offer computer design services. The process differs from store to store, and not all branches of those chains promoting computer-assisted design actually offer the service.

One approach has the customer sit down in front of a computer display terminal manned by a trained operator and view different appliances and cabinet styles. The computer moves the kitchen components around until the customer approves their arrangement.

At this point, it prints out a floor plan plus appropriate elevations. In the do-it-yourself oriented home centers, the computer also prints out a materials list and cutting list (a list of the dimensions to which the boards must be cut), complete with prices so the customer knows immediately how much the project will cost. Whether the customer gets to keep the plans and lists should he or she decide not to buy varies from chain to chain.

In another approach, the customer never sees the computer. Instead, a salesperson calls on the customer at home. He takes measurements of the existing kitchen and has the customer fill out a questionnaire that is an abbreviated form of the wish list. This information is fed into the computer, which generates plans, elevations and a set of construction specifications. Sometimes two alternative designs are provided. To help close the sale, the computer can also generate a rendering of the plan. Customers can examine this design data, but can't keep anything unless they sign a contract with the store, which then offers to act as the general contractor.

In both cases, the salespeople who take the customer information are there primarily to make a sale. They may or may not have any formal design training. But in both cases the computer-assisted design service is usually offered free.

One budget item consistently overlooked by owners who remodel their kitchens is the cost of living with the disruption until the project is finished. For example, you must figure in the cost of eating all your meals out for as long as the project takes to complete. Doing this for a family of four over a 6-week period can add up to a hefty sum.

The trick to keeping within a realistic budget is to determine what you can afford, then to stick with your decisions. You should also consider the impact of the project on the value of your house. A well-designed and well-equipped kitchen is an attractive feature when it comes time to sell, but it's possible to over-improve your house relative to your neighborhood. You should refer any questions you have about this to a real estate expert.

One way to keep costs down is to act as your own contractor and also to do part of the work yourself. As your own contractor, you will have to buy all the materials and arrange for their delivery. A lumber yard catering to professionals, as opposed to a home-center store, will estimate materials for you based on your plans. Since lumber prices vary from yard to yard, take your plans to several stores to get the best price and delivery schedule. Remember, they regard you, the remodeler, as a one-time buyer and will give delivery preference to their regular customers, so give your material suppliers ample notice of when you want deliveries made. It's false economy to pay less for materials that cannot be delivered when you need them.

When buying materials, make sure to add a percentage for wastage, for unexpected contingencies and for mistakes. Generally wastage is figured at 15 percent. What this really means is you'll have to buy 15 percent more material than called for by the plans. For detailing and finish work, such as laying an intricately patterned tile floor, plan for even more wastage.

Other tasks you face as your own contractor are hiring subcontractors, such as carpenters, plumbers and electricians, and making sure they complete their jobs according to the construction schedule—which you must establish and adhere to.

A kitchen remodeling may require a building permit. It's your responsibility to get a permit, if necessary. A permit carries with it the obligation of having the work inspected by the building department. They will tell you what inspections are necessary, which you must schedule with the appropriate inspector.

Doing The Work Yourself

If you plan to do some of the work yourself, you shoulder an added burden, and you shouldn't take it on without a lot of thought. Look carefully at your plans. If the project involves complex carpentry,

The Design Council

Left: **Custom storage racks designed to fit individual cabinets can greatly increase storage capacity by making use of otherwise wasted space. Rack units usually pull out, making stored items more accessible.**

Below: **Ceramic tile isn't just for floors. Its tough surface is ideal for counters and back splashes. The only drawback is that grout lines between the tiles collect dirt and food particles, and cleaning them can be tedious.**

Courtesy of American Olean Tile Co.

think twice about tackling that part of the job unless you have previous building experience—and the right tools.

If you opt to do work yourself, you must make a firm commitment to put in the time necessary to complete it. If you have a full-time job with regular hours, this can be a difficult commitment to make. And remodeling your kitchen on weekends is definitely a bad mistake, as you'll find your project extending limitlessly into the future.

There are, however, many jobs ideally suited to the do-it-yourselfer—demolition, for example. Before you can put the new kitchen in, you have to take out the old one. Doing the tear-out yourself can save hundreds of dollars.

A new kitchen will probably need new electrical wiring, and this is also a job you can handle with a minumum of difficulty. If you do this work yourself, buy one of the several good how-to books that explain basic electrical wiring and follow the directions for adding new branch circuits. With electricity, safety counts for everything, so make sure the power is switched off at the panel when you connect new branch circuits.

Your present kitchen probably doesn't have enough power to support new appliances. Today's National Electric Code requires that you install two 20-amp branch circuits to handle small appliances. This is only common sense. It eliminates the aggravation of not being able to make coffee and toast simulta-

neously. However, if you plan a gadget-rich kitchen, you should probably install a third 20-amp circuit to handle the additional load.

The remaining do-it-yourself jobs tend to group at the end of the project: tasks such as laying tile or sheet flooring, painting and hanging wallcovering. By the time the work has progressed to a point where finishing work

can begin, the appliances should be installed and working, the electrical circuits energized and running water restored. This means that you and your family can pick up the threads of normal life again. The new kitchen may be messy and look unfinished, but at least you can cook in it, thus diminishing the pressure to quickly complete the final detail work.

Richard S. Mandelkorn

Two ovens allow baking and roasting to be done simultaneously, greatly increasing the kitchen's capability. Twin built-in ovens are a popular option, and standard ovens can be purchased in combination with microwave or convection ovens.

CHAPTER 3
The Hidden Elements of Design

Many people judge a kitchen by its counters and appliances, but other things are just as important for kitchen efficiency—good lighting, proper ventilation and safety. Too often we take these vital elements for granted and only miss them when they're not there.

Lighting

If we can not see, we can not work. Considering the amount of time we spend in our kitchens, good lighting is a must for both comfort and efficiency.

A well-lighted kitchen requires at least 25-foot candles of ambient, or general, illumination. That's the amount of light produced by three 150-watt incandescent bulbs or four 40-watt fluorescent tubes. To do the most good, the general light source should be centrally located and hung either from the ceiling or be recessed into it. A light-colored ceiling maximizes the effect of this illumination by reflecting and scattering light throughout the room. Avoid light fixtures with shading devices that keep the light from striking the ceiling.

General room light should be supplemented with other light fixtures located directly over work surfaces, the range and the sink. A common way to provide specific task lighting is with small, switch-controlled fluorescent fixtures installed under wall cabinets. Give careful thought to locat-

ing these fixtures and how they will best accommodate your particular work habits.

Lights, recessed into a ceiling or soffit, also provide good task light over work surfaces. These fixtures have the added advantage of throwing light onto cabinets. You can also buy accessories for recessed fixtures that allow directional control of the light.

Getting light over a cooktop can be more difficult. While many range hoods have a built-in fixture to accommodate a low-wattage incandescent bulb, this is not enough for proper lighting, A better solution is a recessed fixture in the ceiling above the range, or, if that is impossible, a track light that can be aimed toward the cooking area. If you're remodeling and plan to have an island work area and cooktop, plan to install directional task lighting above it.

If your kitchen has an eating area, don't forget about proper lighting there as well. A decorative hanging fixture, controlled by a dimmer switch, can give this area an intimate feel, and still allow you the option of turning the light to full power for those times when the eating table has to double as a food preparation surface.

Ventilation

There's nothing like awakening to the smell of sizzling bacon and brewing coffee. But what smells appetizing at 8 in the morning is stale by mid-afternoon. Without proper

ventilation your kitchen will provide an unwanted workout for your sense of smell. More important, it's imperative to remove the moisture generated by cooking; otherwise, it will cause damage to wall and ceiling finishes, and, if it infiltrates behind the drywall into the stud spaces, it could eventually lead to mildew and rot in the wall itself.

The most effective way to remove moisture and cooking odors is to have a ventilating hood directly above the

cooktop or range. Two types of hood are available: those that vent directly to the outside by means of a duct and those without ducts that pass odor- and moisture-laden air through a filtering system before recycling the air back into the kitchen. Ducted systems are preferable because they also remove heat, but in many kitchens, especially those in apartments or townhouses that share common walls, it isn't practical to install the outside duct.

Safety Tips for Commercial Ranges

If you're installing a commercial-type gas range, common sense and counter space isn't enough to ensure proper safety.

Six-burner commercial ranges generate substantially more heat than a standard consumer range. Heat output is measured in British Thermal Units (BTUs) per hour and a typical household range will put out approximately 10,000 BTUs per hour, per burner. By contrast, a commercial range puts out roughly 20,000 BTUs per burner. With the increased heat comes a greater risk of fire. That's why restaurant installations are strictly controlled by fire-prevention regulations and building codes.

Play it safe; if you're buying one for your kitchen, talk to your building department. They can tell you how far the range must be from combustible materials—cabinets, wood walls, etc. Think in the same safety terms you would if you were installing a wood-burning stove in your living room and seriously consider finishing adjacent walls in tile or stainless steel. Also, restaurant installations must be sprinklered, a total impracticality in a house, but the inference is clear. Keep a good fire extinguisher handy.

A final point to remember if you're installing a commercial range: They weigh more than normal stoves. Make sure that your floor can support the added weight. In older houses, this might mean doubling the floor joists below the range, especially if the spans are long or if the old joists have been notched to accommodate pipes and ductwork.

Photo: Daniel Eifert; Design: Lyn Petersen/Motif Designs

In this commercial range installation, a large soffit houses the exhaust motor and ducts but also works as a key design element— its red-and-white grid work complementing the tile patterned wall-covering.

Whatever system you choose, make sure that it has the capacity to move 100 cubic feet of air per minute for each lineal foot of hood length. This is a minimum requirement for good kitchen ventilation. Many range and cooktop manufacturers market products that include an exhaust fan. These built-in fans are designed to duct to the outside. But, with some models, the effectiveness decreases as the duct length increases because the blower motor lacks the necessary power to push air beyond a given distance. This could be a potential problem if your cooktop is slated for a kitchen island that necessitates a long duct running under the floor to an outside wall. Before buying one of these models, make sure it will work properly in your kitchen plan.

There are instances when you will need greater ventilating capacity. For example, if you are installing a restaurant-style range whose burners produce almost twice as much heat as those of a normal household range, you should install an exhaust fan with a substantially greater capacity. Range manufacturers can provide you with the recommended exhaust capacity needed to accommodate your particular model.

Another place to check is your local building department. Commercial installation of restaurant ranges is controlled by code, and while, as a homeowner, you may not have to conform to the applicable code, it will provide you with valuable guidelines for a safe installation.

Another device for good kitchen ventilation is a window. Make sure that kitchen windows open easily, and, if you are planning a remodeling in which you'll tear out walls, consider adding another window to create a natural pattern of cross ventilation through the room.

Safety

Most home accidents occur in the kitchen. While safety is primarily a matter of good judgment and common sense, there are design features you can build into your kitchen to make it a safer environment for you and your children.

Burns are the most common kitchen accident. In a typical scenario the cook loses his or her grip on a pot while removing it from the cooktop. The resulting juggling act to regain control causes the contents to spill and scald the cook.

To minimize the possibility

Photo: Robert Perron; Design: Louis MacKall

Robert Perron

Facing page: This custom-made copper hood holds a ductless exhaust fan. In ductless systems, air is passed through charcoal filters to remove grease and odors before being reintroduced into the kitchen. While not as effective as systems that vent odors to the outside (since the air is recycled, not replaced), it is the only option in many kitchens.

Above: Besides being a functional surface, tile creates a hominess that's grown increasingly popular as various country styles enjoy renewed popularity. When buying ceramic tile for a kitchen, choose tiles with a matte finish, as they will retain some traction when wet. High gloss tiles, on the other hand, become slippery, creating a safety hazard.

of this kind of accident, provide an accessible set-down spot for hot pans next to the cooking surface. This counter space should be at least 15 inches wide. For maximum safety, there should be 15 inches of space on either side of the cooktop. People bumping into pots as they cook on burners is another cause of burn accidents. Rambunctious children are especially prone to this kind of mishap. To reduce the chance of this happening, swivel the pot handles out of the way of kitchen traffic. The 15-inch set-down counters next to the cooktop will give you the space to do this. If your remodeling plans call for a cooktop located on an island, but the island cannot provide the 15-inch counters without restricting the space in the rest of your kitchen, you should consider an alternative plan.

Built-in ovens are both practical and attractive, but in many kitchens they are positioned away from counters. It's just as important to provide a set-down spot for roasting pans coming out of the oven as it is for pots on the cooktop. Position a 15-inch counter close to any built-in oven for this purpose.

Range-top fire is another potential hazard. Burning grease and other fats cannot be extinguished with water, so for safety, mount a chemical compound fire extinguisher near the cooking area. Today's kitchen extinguishers no longer resemble the ominous red bombs of yesteryear. Several manufacturers offer models designed to mount inconspicuously.

Household chemicals are another potential danger. Too often they are routinely stored under the sink in a cabinet that's accessible to children. Common sense dictates that rodent poisons, cleaning solutions and caustic substances be kept out of a child's reach. Wall cabinets above a refrigerator provide a much safer location for these substances. If this isn't practical, consider a floor-to-ceiling cupboard or pantry and set aside a high shelf for chemical storage.

Counters and floors should be planned with safety in mind. Avoid sharp corners on countertops and islands that tend to be at eye level for young children. Pick a floor material that doesn't lose its traction when wet. This is especially important if you will be entering your kitchen through a back door. Wet shoes and an armful of groceries are a sure recipe for a fall if your floor surface is slick.

Facing page: **Traditional kitchen design, whenever possible, placed the sink below a window to provide a view of the outside. Enlarging an existing window or adding new ones is an easy and inexpensive remodeling option.**

Below: **A set-down area for pots and pans hot out of the oven is vital to kitchen safety. When it's not possible to provide set-down space next to the oven, a pull-out, heat-resistant board is a good alternative.**

Photo: Karen Bussolini

CHAPTER 4
Appliances

Put together, appliances form the engine that makes your kitchen run smoothly and efficiently. Out of date appliances or ones that no longer work properly can turn kitchen chores into pure drudgery; for any new or remodeled kitchen, you should put a high priority on acquiring modern appliances.

If you want only the bare basics, all you really need is a refrigerator and a range, but most people would agree that a dishwasher is mandatory. From there on, it's a question of personal preference. There's an almost endless selection of convenience appliances to choose from, the final choice depending on your budget and how big your kitchen is. If garbage bothers you, there are trash compactors. For quick food preparation, there are microwaves, available in individual units or in combination with wall ovens. You can also buy microwave–convection oven combination units. For year-round barbecuing, there are indoor grills built into cooktops, complete with efficient exhaust fans.

There are also the small countertop kitchen appliances, always plugged in, waiting for the command to make toast, bake a single potato, whip up a meringue or brew a cup of coffee. Even these old standbys have been updated as manufacturers introduce compact under-cabinet mounted appliances: miniature microwaves, toaster ovens, electric knives and can

Courtesy of General Electric

Left: The trend in small appliances is toward miniaturization. Small units, such as this microwave, are designed to mount below cabinets, thus keeping countertops free for kitchen tasks.

Facing page: The top-of-the-line American refrigerator, besides providing almost 23 cubic feet of storage, is loaded with conveniences such as an ice maker, cold water dispenser and quick-access door for cold drinks. But the operating cost is high, averaging about $360 per year for electricity.

The Design Council

Right: Sleek appliances, like this drop-in range, can be used in combination with a country decor to create an efficient yet homey kitchen.

Courtesy of Poggenpohl

Left: Top-of-the-line cabinet manufacturers, such as Poggenpohl, offer appliance garages as a design option. These storage areas can be closed off by tambour doors. In Europe, they can also be wired to provide appliance plug in. Local electrical codes may affect this option in the United States.

openers, automated coffee makers, mixers and so forth.

Individually, none of these appliances, large or small, cost a great deal, given what they do. But together they add up to a hefty cost. To avoid being nickeled and dimed to death on your appliance budget, make an honest assessment of your needs. If you can keep yourself from becoming like the kid in the candy store, you can have a kitchen where the appliances work for you, rather than collect dust after the novelty wears off.

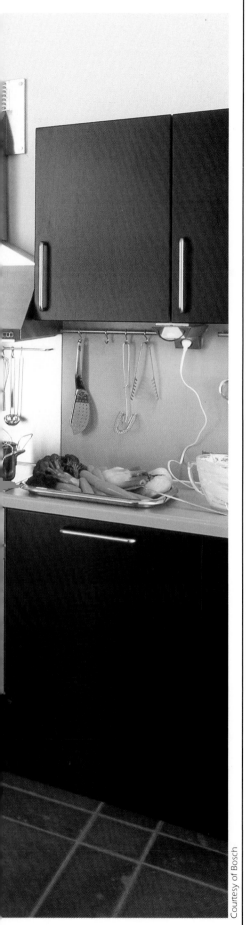

When space and money are no problem, a kitchen can literally include everything. The commercial range handles most of the cooking, but a separate, self-venting grill with its accessory griddle built into the work island is available for fast-food fixes. In this kitchen, much of the storage is in floor-to-ceiling units located in the eating area.

Left: Moveable kitchen carts provide work space when and where it's needed. Most carts have butcher-block surfaces for chopping and food preparation and many have places to store knives, glassware and small pans.

Above: Maximum space utilization is a hallmark of European design. Every nook and cranny has its use; what would have been wasted space in other cabinets is used here to store wine and cookbooks.

John Driemen

The Europeans are Coming

Perhaps because the average European house is smaller than its American counterpart, the scale of European household products tends to be smaller also. European kitchens don't have space for clunky appliances. As a result, European cooktops, ovens, refrigerators and dishwashers are compact to minimize wasted space.

These designs are finally catching on in America, and domestic manufacturers are experiencing the Euro-Style revolution. Much of the heralded change, however, is advertising hype. For example, although the European-style high-tech black glass cooktops are all the rage in big-city kitchen boutiques, American companies continue to make them in traditionally large American sizes. The standard four-burner U.S. cooktop is 36 inches wide; the compact model 30 inches. By comparison, the Europeans can get six burners into the metric equivalent of 36 inches and their compact four-burner unit is less than 24 inches across. European cooktops also combine electric elements with gas burners—a combination that provides maximum versatility to the serious cook. This feature has yet to be offered by an American company.

On the other hand, American manufacturers have discovered the cooking efficiency and easy clean-up features of one-piece cast-iron electric elements. These are gradually replacing American coil and drip pan elements that haven't changed significantly in 60 years.

While American companies promote refrigerator/freezers the size of small cars that provide water, ice and quick access to soda pop, the Europeans offer units, less the bells and whistles, containing equivalent cubic foot storage capacities that take up half the floor space.

It remains to be seen if Americans will abandon the big American models and switch to European compactness the same way they did with cars.

Courtesy of Allmilmö

Above: **European kitchens treat the range vent as a design element that's integral to the overall cabinet plan. The vent shown here provides the required power to ventilate the cooktop and plenty of task lighting for the cook.**

Left: **American appliance makers, such as Jenn-Air, are adding Euro-style cooking elements to their product lines. In some cases, these elements can be retrofitted into older model cooktops.**

Photo: Lea Babcock; Design: Mary Jane Pappas

CHAPTER 5

Surfaces and Storage

Ample and organized storage space for food and utensils is the thread that holds an efficient kitchen together. Without enough storage, you can't keep the items you need close at hand, and without well-organized storage, life in the kitchen can be a never-ending scavenger hunt.

While the amount of storage space you need depends on your lifestyle, there are some general principles you should adhere to when planning the storage space in a new kitchen.

Storage capacity is determined by the linear dimensions of your cabinets. This is sometimes referred to as *running feet*. Cabinets are made in standard sizes, unless you buy top-of-the-line custom-made units sized to your order. Base cabinets (those that sit on the floor, providing the base for your countertops) are typically 34½ inches high without the countertop and 24 inches deep. Width varies in increments of 3 inches. For a bare minimum of storage space, you should have a cabinet run of at least 72 inches.

Full wall cabinets, called *hangers,* are 30 inches high and 12 inches deep. Like base cabinets, their widths vary in 3-inch increments. Wall cabinets are installed so their top edges are 84 inches above the floor. Assuming a standard 36-inch high counter, this results in a 18-inch space between the cabinet bottom and the countertop.

Despite high cost and the need for careful installation, marble is an excellent kitchen countertop material. Expert bakers recommend marble slabs for rolling dough. In this kitchen, glass-door cabinets complement the marble and work with it to form interesting patterns of light and dark. A point to consider about glass doors, however, is that they show dirt and fingerprints more than laminated doors; if you choose them, be prepared for the extra cleaning they require.

Photo: Durston Saylor: Design: Shope, Reno and Wharton

To get the most storage out of a kitchen, you must use small spaces creatively. This space, too narrow for a useful cabinet, is filled with 4 pull-out bins which conveniently keep odds and ends.

The Design Council

The Design Council

This cramped kitchen uses a mobile chopping table to provide a work space that's equidistant from the sink and the oven.

Robert Perron

An alternative to a moveable cart is a pull-out table, either built into the cabinets as shown here or used as part of a sepa-rate unit. When not in use, the work surface stows away, preventing disruption of the kitchen's traffic pattern.

When determining the storage capacity of your kitchen, don't count the space below the sink. This is the logical place for a garbage pail and non-toxic cleaning materials.

Hard-to-reach wall cabinets above the refrigerator or wall oven are best set aside for the storage of seasonal paraphernalia that doesn't receive frequent use and should not be counted as part of the minimum 72-inch cabinet run.

Corner cabinets traditionally are space wasters. This is because they usually have fixed shelves or the door opens so inconveniently that it's difficult to reach to the back of the cabinet. A solution to this situation is to install lazy-Susan-type shelves. For maximum efficiency, these shelves can be incorporated with a "pie-cut door" (an L-shaped door that is attached to a pie cut in the shelves).

Many standard kitchen cabinets have fixed shelves so there is little flexibility for arranging items, and plenty of wasted space. Cabinet systems using vinyl-covered wire shelves, pull-out doors and units designed to convert small closets into pantries improve this, but the price goes up accordingly.

Robert Perron

All too often, kitchen drawers turn into miniature attics—places for odds and ends that you want to keep, because one day they might be needed. Good drawer organization, however, greatly increases storage capacity and improves efficiency.

Below: A picnic bench in a kitchen may seem out of place to some people, but this large table can double as a food preparation area when counter space in the rest of the kitchen is limited.

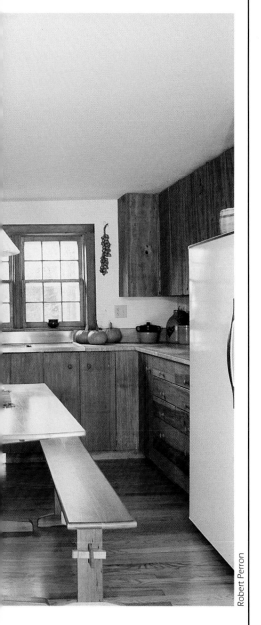

Above: Finding a spot for cookbooks and reference material can require some ingenuity. Installing a magazine rack with doors can solve this problem.

Robert Perron

Robert Perron

Few people think twice about refrigerator location, but not every kitchen includes an open stairway. Because the stairs effectively remove a wall from the kitchen, it's necessary, here, to fit the refrigerator underneath the stair stringers.

J. Michael Kanouff

Combining open storage with traditional cabinets can increase kitchen efficiency. Place often-used items in the open areas for quick access, and use the cabinets to store less-used utensils or seasonal items.

Photo: Lea Babcock; Design: Close Associates

Pull-out bread boards were an early attempt to provide more kitchen work surface. Today's pullouts (*facing page*) are sturdy enough to support heavy cooking pots and can double as small tables for afternoon coffee. This custom table (*below*), with leaves that spread apart like a fan of playing cards, offers unlimited combinations for both food preparation and eating.

Photo: Durston Saylor; Design: Shope. Reno and Wharton

Glass doors set on white cabinets can create exciting contrasts of light and dark. Here they also complement the white-and-black patterned floor.

John Driemen

Right: Open shelves, suspended from the ceiling, provide space for displaying large items or decorative pots and pans that are only used occasionally.

Henrich Blessing

Besides telling you at a glance what you have stored in your cabinets, glass doors also provide the opportunity to show off kitchen collectibles.

Photo: Lea Babcock; Design: Mary Jane Pappas

Facing page: Narrow spaces are ideal for storing canned goods; pull-out shelves make them accessible. Shelf height can be set to accommodate a large variety of foodstuffs. Space above a built-in oven is well suited for tray storage.

This ultimate in kitchen pantry storage features swinging shelf units that fold into each other for maximum use of available space. Units like this are usually custom-made, though some kitchen cabinet manufacturers offer them as options with their more expensive lines.

Less expensive than the unit shown on the preceding page, this pull-out, wire-grid storage system lets you see everything at a glance. Individual shelves can be arranged to accommodate different height items, and accessory grids hold pot lids and other kitchen utensils.

A swing-out pantry can also be installed in base cabinets if there is no satisfactory location for a floor-to-ceiling unit.

This kitchen baking center features a pull-out shelf for the mixer and open shelves to store bowls, utensils and regularly used baking items.

Photo: Lea Babcock; Design: Mary Jane Pappas

Perhaps because European kitchens tend to be smaller than their American counterparts, designers there look for storage space in unexpected locations. The two ideas shown below, both from Poggenpohl, are designed to take advantage of the space between the upper cabinets and the counter. Various storage arrangements are available, and the components are easily removable for cleaning.

Courtesy of Poggenpohl

Courtesy of Poggenpohl

Above: Space-saving under cabinet appliances are an effective use of kitchen back splash space.

The mechanically operated pop-up table for a mixer has been around for a long time. It is still a handy accessory that solves both the where-to-store and where-to-use worries of this appliance.

Courtesy of Wilsonart

A variation of the pop-up mixer table allows for storage of a microwave or convection oven in a work island. When storing appliances this way, consider installing an electrical box and receptacle inside the cabinet for more convenient plug in.

Photo: Lea Babcock; Design: Mary Jane Pappas

Above: Tambour doors, made of closely set wood strips attached to a piece of cloth, are ideal for round cabinets, because they are flexible enough to conform to the curved grooves into which they must fit.

Getting full use of a corner cabinet is a tough problem: a single door means a difficult reach into the corner. If two doors are used they must swing in opposite directions.

The other viable alternative to corner storage is a lazy-Susan unit with a pie-cut door attached to the shelves. The door swings inward when the lazy-Susan opens.

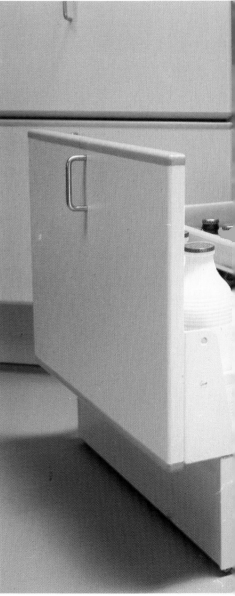

This kitchen takes full advantage of the corner. Rather than a 90-degree junction of 2 cabinet runs, the corner turns at a 45-degree angle to allow installation of cabinets that are fully accessible behind a single swinging door. An appliance garage on the counter completes this well-thought-out storage corner.

A tambour door that recesses into the ceiling gives the option of using shelf space for display or closing it off to prevent stored items from collecting too much dust.

Courtesy of Poggenpohl

Courtesy of Bosch

Again from Europe, where convenience is a way of life, comes this stow-away unit for bottle storage. Designed to fit into a base cabinet, the unit moves on casters so that heavy bottles need only be hand-carried the short distance from car to kitchen.

77

A STEP-BY-STEP GUIDE
Building a Small Swing-Away Spice Rack

Storing spices can be a real test for your kitchen, especially if you don't care for the glitzy rack and jar combinations sold at kitchen boutiques. But lining up your spice jars on a cabinet shelf is a waste of space.

Building and installing this hinged spice organizer lets you put every inch of kitchen storage space to good use, and because it swings out of the way, it won't impede access to the other items stored behind it in the cabinet.

Start by choosing the cabinet where you want to keep your spices. You'll have to cut back the existing shelves by about 6 inches to accommodate the organizer. If your shelves are adjustable, remove them and cut them to the proper dimensions on a table saw or with a hand-held circular saw. It's a good idea to take off an additional ½ inch to ensure proper clearance for the rack when it's installed. To support the narrower shelves, move the standards back or bore new holes for the shelf support pins. If shelves are fixed, you should build the rack to fit between them.

For a custom fit of the new rack, measure the space where you intend to hang it both left to right and top to bottom. Allow a ½-inch clearance on both top and bottom. You must also allow about 1½ inches of clear space left to right so the rack can swing open without hitting the cabinet frame. This clearance de-

Robert Perron

pends, of course, on the length and depth of the rack.

To test the accuracy of your measurements, cut a piece of paper to the size of one of the shelves in your proposed rack. Now hold the paper at one corner and pivot it to see how much clearance you'll need on the opposite edge. Adjust the dimensions of your rack accordingly and cut the pieces from either 1-by-6- or 1-by-8-inch clear pine.

Assemble the rack (as shown in illustration) using glued butt joints and countersunk 1¼-inch No. 6 flathead wood screws. Fill the holes with wood putty, sand with 150-grit sandpaper, then coat with clear satin polyurethane. After the first coat dries, sand with 220-grit sandpaper and then apply a second coat of polyurethane.

Cut a *continuous hinge*, sometimes called a *piano hinge*, to the correct length with a hacksaw and hold it in place against the cabinet; mark and bore pilot holes. Now attach the hinge to the rack using ⅝-inch No. 5 wood screws. Complete the installation by screwing the hinge to the cleat. If the hinge cleat is used, cut it to proper length, and then glue it to the cabinet side, positioning it flush with the opening. For added strength, screw it down with 2-inch No. 8 flathead wood screws.

To keep the rack from unintentionally swinging out, install a magnetic catch according to the directions on the package.

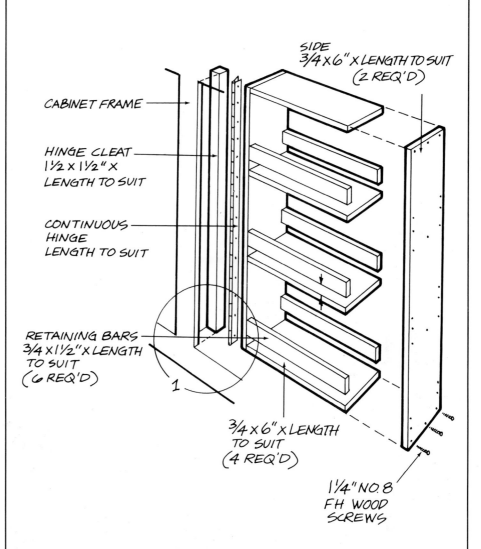

SIDE
3/4 x 6" x LENGTH TO SUIT
(2 REQ'D)

CABINET FRAME

HINGE CLEAT
1½ x 1½" x
LENGTH TO SUIT

CONTINUOUS
HINGE
LENGTH TO SUIT

RETAINING BARS
3/4 x 1½" x LENGTH
TO SUIT
(6 REQ'D)

1

3/4 x 6" x LENGTH
TO SUIT
(4 REQ'D)

1¼" NO. 8
FH WOOD
SCREWS

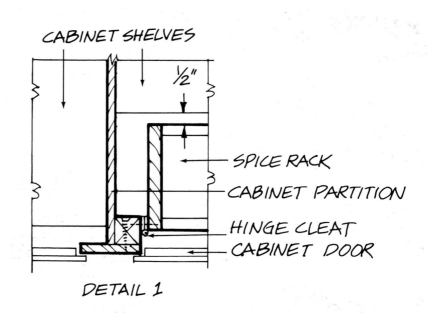

CABINET SHELVES

½"

SPICE RACK

CABINET PARTITION

HINGE CLEAT

CABINET DOOR

DETAIL 1

Photo: Durston Saylor; Design: Shope, Reno and Wharton

CHAPTER 6
Floors

Kitchen floors take a pounding. Not only are they subjected to the heaviest and most constant household traffic, but they have to survive spills, dropped pots and pans, broken plates and glasses. If your kitchen has a back door that's regularly used, you can count on dirt, mud and water being ground into your kitchen floor on a regular basis.

For many people, a kitchen floor is synonymous with linoleum, even though it's no longer manufactured, having been replaced by vinyl sheet flooring. These new vinyl floors never need waxing and clean up easily with a mop, making them an ideal low-maintenance kitchen floor material, especially for families with children.

Leading manufacturers of vinyl sheet flooring offer patterns that faithfully reproduce the look of expensive tile, imported marble and even wood parquet. Installing this flooring is easy because it lays flat without requiring an adhesive. Old flooring can be left in place except when it's too badly damaged or gouged to allow the new vinyl floor to lay flush on top of it. Because of its natural resiliency, vinyl flooring is easy on the feet. It also absorbs shocks, thus reducing the likelihood of breakage when a glass or plate is accidentally dropped.

Ceramic or quarry tile is another popular kitchen floor covering, although more expensive than vinyl flooring. When choosing tile, remem-

Courtesy of Armstrong World Industries, Inc.

Vinyl sheet flooring can simulate patterns ranging from marble to parquet. Easy to clean, its resiliency provides a comfortable surface for prolonged standing and reduces the likelihood of breakage if something is dropped.

Ceramic tile is the decorator's choice when a generous budget allows for its significantly higher cost.

Courtesy of Kitchen Aid

Phillip Ennis

Choosing a light-colored flooring increases the amount of light in a kitchen, because it reflects and amplifies the light put out by general illumination fixtures. Light-colored tiles also make a small room seem larger.

ber that a matte finish will provide more traction than a polished glaze, especially when the floor is wet.

If you're remodeling with tile, the old flooring will have to be ripped out. However, because tile is usually installed with a thin-set bonding agent such as an organic adhesive or a latex-portland cement mortar bed, minor variations in floor level can be corrected by changing the thickness of the thin-set.

While tile has many of the easy-to-clean features of vinyl flooring, it is harder on the feet and individual tiles can break if a heavy object is dropped on them. Also, since tiles are bonded to the subfloor, any shifting or settling of the house can cause cracks to develop across the tiles.

If your kitchen design calls for a wood floor, select a hardwood, such as oak or maple. Soft woods like pine are prone to nicks and dents. Wood boards are almost always milled for tongue-and-groove installation and a blind nailing technique. Using standard boards such as 1-by-4s or 1-by-6s and butting them together to create an Early American look may be aesthetically pleasing, but the gaps between the boards will increase as the boards dry and shrink. These natural crevices become dirt traps.

Any wood floor should be sealed with several coats of polyurethane. This will provide an easy-to-clean surface that won't need any more attention than vinyl or tile. However, over time the polyurethane will yellow, so choosing a wood floor is a conscious commitment to periodic sanding and refinishing.

Peter Paige

Laying Vinyl Sheet Flooring

Laying vinyl sheet flooring is an easy do-it-yourself project, because today's rolled floorings don't require adhesive and, in most cases, can be installed directly over the old floor.

Rolled flooring is sold in 12-foot-wide rolls with the length cut to your order. In most rooms, this means a seamless installation with a single piece of flooring.

To lay flooring, you'll need the following tools: tape measure, metal straightedge, heavy duty scissors, utility knife, hammer, screwdriver, handsaw, putty knife and a scrap piece of 2-by-4 for fitting the flooring into corners.

Before starting, remove the furniture and any other moveable objects. Take off the baseboards and any floor trim or molding. Vacuum the old floor. Any holes in the old floor should be filled with a latex floor patching compound before installing the new floor, and you may have to install a 3/8-inch plywood sub-floor if the old floor is in very bad shape.

Courtesy of Armstrong World Industries, Inc.

Courtesy of Mannington Resilient Floors

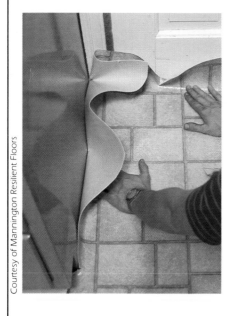

1 In another room, unroll the flooring and cut it to the rough dimensions of the room in which it is to be installed, leaving 3 to 6 inches of extra flooring on all sides. Trial fit the flooring before making any trim cuts.

2 Use a handsaw to cut an 1/8-inch slot in the molding to allow the flooring to fit snugly underneath.

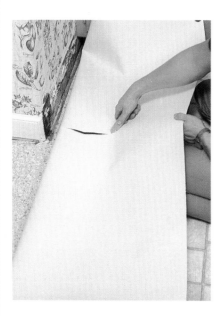

3 Use a utility knife to cut the vinyl sheet flooring to fit around the corners.

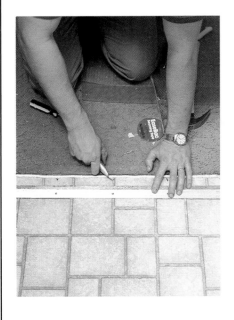

4 Corner fitting is easier when excess flooring is trimmed at an angle that terminates at a corner.

7 Use a metal threshold at the point where vinyl flooring ends and another floor surface begins. Make sure to leave excess flooring and install the threshold before trimming.

5 Seam sealer, supplied by the flooring manufacturer, hides any joints between pieces of vinyl flooring.

8 Nail or screw the threshold over the seam between the two flooring materials.

6 Use adhesive tape to secure the vinyl to the old flooring at the points where it joins another flooring material and at the points where it will be covered by a metal threshold.

9 Use a putty knife to pressure fit the flooring when you reinstall the trim work.

John Schwartz

CHAPTER 7
Walls

all finishes are an important part of kitchen decor, but if you want them to last, they must also be easy to clean and resistant to repeated scrubbing. Even with the best ventilation, you can expect grease build-ups on kitchen walls, especially on those near the cooktop or range. Cooking also generates moisture in the form of steam, so wall finishes must be able to stand up to this as well.

Paint

Because of its ease of application and its ability to withstand repeated cleanings with typical household solvents, semigloss enamel paint is the most commonly selected kitchen wall finish. Enamel paints are available in both latex and alkyd bases. There is little difference in quality between equivalently priced latex and alkyd enamels. Professional painters prefer alkyd paints because they cover better than latex and show fewer brush marks, but cleanup requires a solvent such as turpentine. Most do-it-yourselfers opt for the latex paints because brushes and rollers can be cleaned with water.

No matter what type of paint you select, prime any new walls and ceilings with a good quality primer-sealer. This not only provides a good tooth (a surface that promotes adhesion) for the finish coat of enamel, but will protect the drywall from moisture infiltration, thus reducing the possi-

Robert Perron

bility of annoying rot or mildew problems later on.

While paint color is a matter of personal taste, it's best to select light shades that will amplify and reflect the light. On the other hand, pure white can cause glare, resulting in possible eye strain, so one of the many off-white shades is probably a more appropriate choice.

Wallcovering

With the increasing popularity of colonial and American country styles, wallcovering (wallpaper) is back in vogue for kitchen wall finishes. However, special care must be taken in selecting it since not all wallcovering is moisture resistant or even cleanable. The

Photo: Daniel Eifert; Design: Rubén de Saavedra

Facing page: Shoji screens are decorative Japanese room dividers and are seldom seen in traditionally styled American kitchens. Here a Shoji screen accents a particularly tiny kitchen while functioning as a slider for a serving pass-through to the dining room.

Wallcovering, or wallpaper, offers an unlimited selection of colors and patterns and is a good alternative to paint. However, wallcovering is best used away from cooking areas where grease splatters, spills and steam can cause stains.

Courtesy of Levolor Lorentzen

Windows not only let in light, their shades can provide a strong graphic element in your overall kitchen design. Modern venetian-type slat shades such as those manufactured by Kirsch and Levolor can be custom ordered in any number of color combinations.

best choices are the vinyl-coated or all-vinyl papers. Properly installed, these coverings are impervious to moisture and relatively easy to clean. Do not, however, put them near the range, cooktop or anywhere you expect grease splatters. A better use of wallcovering is to create decorative accents in areas away from the cooking center, such as the preparation or eating area.

When installing wallcovering, new walls should be sealed and primed in the same manner as for paint. If the wallcovering is hung over a painted wall, make sure the old paint is cleaned and scrubbed to remove any dirt and grime. Otherwise, the wallcovering will not adhere as it should.

Wood

In spite of its inherent rustic beauty, wood should be used only as a decorative element in kitchens rather than as a principal wall finish, because untreated wood absorbs moisture, grease and odors, and it cannot be washed. Any bare wood in a kitchen should be treated with several coats of polyurethane sealer, and you can expect to have to reseal the wood at shorter intervals than you would normally have to repaint.

Tile

The easiest way to add a decorative accent to a wall is with ceramic tile. Fully tiled walls can be stunning in the right kitchen, but tile is the most expensive wall finish available. Some imported tiles cost as much as $20 a square foot. Installation is usually done with a thin-set mastic adhesive, the gaps between tiles grouted. Wall tile is easy to maintain because splatters wipe off the glazed finishes, but cleaning the grout can be an arduous task. It's best, therefore, to choose a dark-colored grout color that won't show dirt and grime.

Choose tile sizes to match the scale of your kitchen. For large rooms, 10-by-10-inch tiles look best. As square footage decreases, reduce tile size progressively to 8-by-8, 6-by-6 or even 4-by-4 inches.

A STEP-BY-STEP GUIDE
Stenciling

A creative alternative to wallcovering is stenciling a pattern onto a painted wall. It's also a good do-it-yourself project. In Colonial times, stenciling was considered an acceptable substitute for wallcovering by money-conscience homeowners. Known today as *Colonial stenciling,* this style consists of a pattern of geometric shapes or stylized fruits and flowers. Craft stores sell kits with which you can reproduce many of the original Colonial patterns at home yourself.

There is another stenciling technique that's more elaborate and results in more representational, less stylized designs. Called either *European* or *continental stenciling,* it relies on multiple stencils, overlayed on each other, to create intricate color shading and a more lifelike appearance. In fact, wallpaper was originally handmade using this kind of stenciling technique. There are books on stenciling available that explain this technique in step-by-step fashion if you want to try it yourself.

Robert Perron

1 Garden books, available in libraries, are a good source of floral designs you can turn into stencil patterns. You don't need to be an artist; just lay tracing paper over the design and outline it with a heavy pencil.

Robert Perron

2 After tracing, use colored pencils to detail the shades of the pattern. The pencils should be the same colors you plan to use for the finished stencil.

3 Transfer the tracing to 6-millimeter Mylar film (sold in art supply stores). This material makes a durable stencil. Cut the pattern out of the Mylar with a matte knife or other sharp cutting tool. Remember, you must cut a separate stencil for each color you apply.

Robert Perron

4 Before starting, dirty each stencil by dabbing it in the color you intend to use it with. This ensures a cleaner line when you apply the stencil to the wall.

Robert Perron

5 Stenciling paints contain a quick dry agent called Japan Dryer. For this agent to work, remove the excess paint from the brushes by dabbing them on paper before making the stencil.

6 Stenciling brushes are round with the most common diameters being 1 inch and 1/2 inch. The brushes are used to apply color over the stenciled pattern.

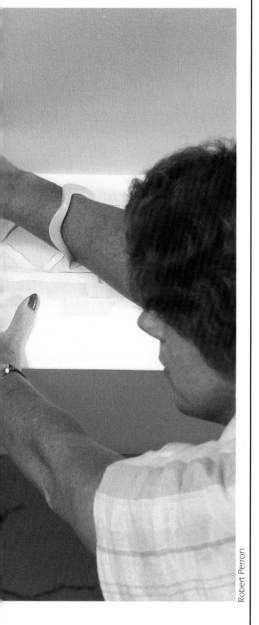

Robert Perron

7 Use smaller brushes to paint intricate colored lines and to create shading effects.

CHAPTER 8

Details and Finishing Touches

R e m o d e l i n g shouldn't focus exclusively on creating an efficient design to showcase the latest appliances. Kitchens must also be comfortable rooms, and much of this comfort is measured by the personal little details that add charm, warmth and livability.

In Chapter 2 we discussed lighting, but our point there was to show how to provide sufficient artificial light to work by. There is also the natural light provided by windows. Many older kitchens have only a single window, usually above the sink. It is there because building codes required it. Its placement can be attributed to the need to provide a pleasant view while doing an unpleasant task—washing dishes.

Adding windows is the simplest structural remodeling project you can undertake and the resulting atmospheric effect on the room is often overwhelming in relation to the minimal installation costs. In addition to windows, you can bring character to your kitchen by installing greenhouses and/or skylights. Greenhouses, especially, bring the outdoors in and make it part of the kitchen. Light provided by large areas of glass gives any room a bright and airy quality, thus making it a more enjoyable room to be in.

Many homemakers like a space in the kitchen set aside for administrative tasks, like paying bills, organizing shopping lists and keeping track of family activities. Such a space

Courtesy of Motif Designs

Curtains are an inexpensive way to add decorative elements to any kitchen. They can either match or accent the paint scheme. Because of their low price, they can be changed whenever you want to alter the look of your kitchen.

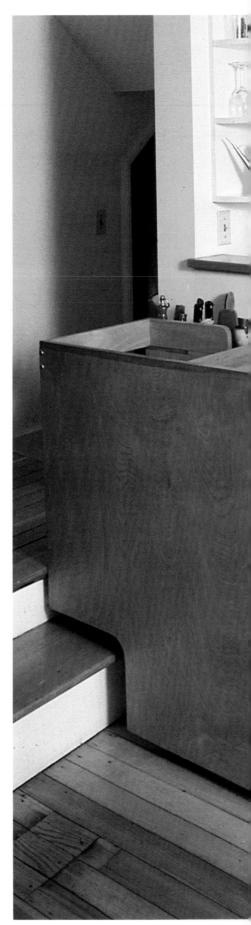

This one-of-a-kind rolling kitchen island, made by a New England craftsman, is designed to store against stair risers. A multifunction unit, it has interchangeable surfaces for cutting, dough rolling and table-side salad preparation.

Robert Perron

can be as simple as a lowered counter with a kneehole to accommodate a chair or as sophisticated as a mini-office complete with computer and communications center.

Another luxury more Americans want in their kitchen is a place in the kitchen to store wine. And as the appeal of gourmet cooking grows, more cooks are buying professional quality pots and pans, which have a certain decorative value even when not in use.

Like choosing a style for your kitchen, the question of detailing is very much a matter of personal taste. But because many kitchen details, such as a display rack for pots, are not expensive, you may want to consider including those things that are the mark of your own personality.

Racks and wall-mounted grids are popular accessories for keeping smaller utensils in a ready-to-use state. Wood racks can be made with strips of lath. "S" hooks are the common way to hang items, though knife holders and plate racks should be securely screwed into any wooden rack.

The Design Council

Courtesy of Quakermaid

A kitchen office needn't resemble an impersonal corporate cubicle. Many cabinet manufacturers offer desk-type units, styled to match the rest of your cabinets. Another alternative is to use a favorite old desk or secretary. A qualified kitchen designer will have no problem incorporating existing accessories or cabinets into the new design.

A kitchen planning center is a logical place for a home computer where it can be used to keep track of household budgets, phone numbers, schedules and recipes. If you include a planning area in your new kitchen, consider adding an additional branch circuit to handle the electrical needs. Code requires that kitchens have two 20-amp circuits for small appliances, but this may not be enough for a computer, printer, telephone answering machine, etc.

Wet bars are popular options with people who like to entertain. They usually include a small sink and a refrigerator designed to fit into a base cabinet.

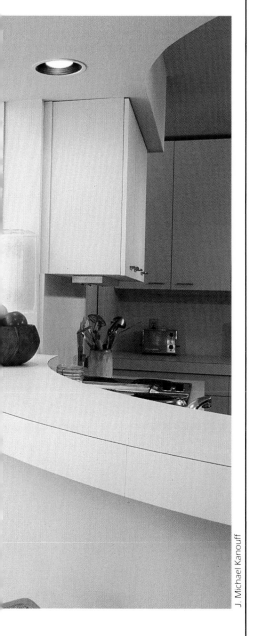

J. Michael Kanouff

Courtesy of Formica Corp.

Facing page: For people who want everything behind closed doors, use one of the pull-out work surfaces discussed earlier, adapting it to recess behind vertically operating tambour doors, as shown here.

Below: For kitchens that include a wet bar, a convenient and different way to store liquor bottles is to employ an English pub-style dispensing bar. Bottles are stored upside down and out of the way, and the dispenser automatically measures out the right amount for a single drink.

Courtesy of Bosch

Alternatives for knife storage are slots cut into the work surface, which are especially easy to construct if you're working with butcher block.

Magnetic racks are a good way to store knives and other sharp objects out of the reach of small children. However, be aware that some knives are too heavy for a magnetic rack. They might stay put for awhile, but vibrations or inadvertent bumping will cause them to fall off.

John Driemen

For almost 40 years, American sinks have featured a faucet with a separate sprayer to rinse dishes. In Europe, both functions are combined in a single fixture. These stylish and practical faucets are becoming increasingly popular in America. On this model, a Grohe Lady Lux, a single mixing valve controls hot and cold water. A control on the pull-out spout sets the spray pattern.

John Driemen

Courtesy of Velox-America, Inc.

Because this balcony kitchen overlooks living spaces below, the only way to ensure natural light is to install skylights.

Brick and rough finished wood are two materials that give a kitchen a traditional country look. Once thought to be too folksy for people's tastes, the American country look is enjoying a resurgence of popularity.

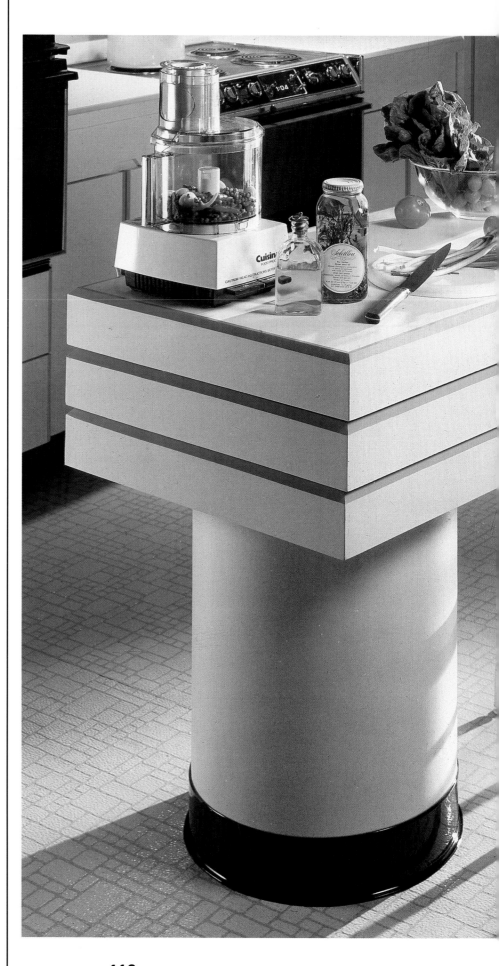

This all-purpose kitchen island opens to triple the work surface, providing space for food preparation, eating or for use as a desk. To see how the island opens, turn to page 63.

Courtesy of Poggenpohl

Some cooks prefer to work seated. Normal base cabinet height, with countertop, is 36 inches, but 28 to 30 inches is a better desktop working height.

Courtesy of Armstrong World Industries, Inc.

STEP-BY-STEP GUIDE
Building A Wine Rack

Americans' taste for wine is increasing, especially since good quality wines from California are priced for cost-conscious budgets. If wine collecting is important to you, or you just want a good selection on hand, you need a place to store the bottles. While we're not suggesting that a temperature and humidity controlled wine cellar is *de rigeur* for the well-equipped kitchen, proper storage is important for the taste of even modest wines.

Too many people stick the wine into kitchen crannies that have proven unsuitable for anything else: typically above a refrigerator or built-in oven. These places should be avoided because heat generated by the appliances can spoil the wine after a period of time.

As an alternative, the wine storage system shown here, which includes space to keep glasses, fits into an existing closet or pantry cabinet unit. It can also be freestanding.

The choice of material depends on personal taste. For the best results use ¾-inch birch veneer plywood (buy three 4-by-8-foot sheets) that can be stained or painted. Three-quarter-inch particle board costs less and works just as well, but looks more utilitarian.

Robert Perron

1. Cut the 4 vertical panels and the top and the bottom pieces from 4-by-8-foot stock using either a table saw or a circle saw. (Note: for this project, any saw used should be mounting a plywood blade.)

2. Cut the ¾-by-6½-inch slots in the vertical panels using the illustration as your guide. If you haven't got a table saw, use a sabre saw.

3. To make the 3 glass and 8 bottle partitions and the shelf, cut a cardboard template matching the dimensions given in the drawing. Use the template to trace out the partitions on a 4-by-8-foot sheet of stock. Cut them out using a table saw or sabre saw.

4. Sand all slots and grooves, first with medium 100-grit sandpaper and then with 150-grit finishing paper.

5. Paint, stain or otherwise finish all components at this point.

6. Assemble the unit by screwing the vertical panels to the top and bottom pieces. Use 1½-inch flathead screws. Drill pilot holes with a ¹⁄₁₆-inch bit.

7. Insert the bottle and glass partitions. They need not be glued.

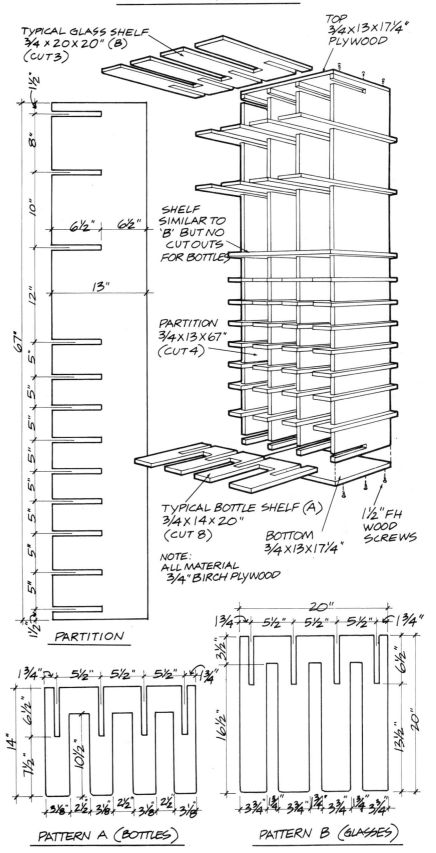

WINE RACK CLOSET INSERT

TYPICAL GLASS SHELF ¾ × 20 × 20" (B) (CUT 3)

TOP ¾ × 13 × 17¼" PLYWOOD

SHELF SIMILAR TO 'B' BUT NO CUT OUTS FOR BOTTLES

PARTITION ¾ × 13 × 67" (CUT 4)

TYPICAL BOTTLE SHELF (A) ¾ × 14 × 20" (CUT 8)

BOTTOM ¾ × 13 × 17¼"

1½" FH WOOD SCREWS

NOTE: ALL MATERIAL ¾" BIRCH PLYWOOD

PARTITION

PATTERN A (BOTTLES)

PATTERN B (GLASSES)

121

Sources
and Index

The manufacturers listed below are representative of those that sell kitchen related building materials and products. Unfortunately, space doesn't allow us to list all manufacturers or all products.

These manufacturers can direct you to retail sales outlets in your area; many of them will also send free catalogs and brochures.

APPLIANCES

Admiral Corporation
1701 East Woodfield Road
Schaumberg, IL 60172

AEG Appliances
c/o Andi-Co
2100 North Central Road
Suite 301
Fort Lee, NJ 07024

Amana Refrigeration Inc.
Amana, IA 52204

Black and Decker
U.S. Household Products
6 Armstrong Road
Shelton, CT 06484

Broan Manufacturing
Company, Inc.
926 West State Street
Hartford, WI 53027

Frigidaire Division of GMC
300 Taylor Street
Dayton, OH 45442

General Electric Company
Customer Relations
Building 6   Room 143
Appliance Park
Louisville, KY 40225

Hotpoint
Customer Relations
Building 6   Room 143
Appliance Park
Louisville, KY 40225

In-Sink-Erator
Division of Emerson
Electric Company
4700 21st Street
Racine, WI 53406

Jenn-Air Corporation
3035 Shadeland Avenue
Indianapolis, IN 46226

Kelvinator Appliance
Company
4248 Kalamazoo SE
Grand Rapids, MI 49508

Kenmore, Sears, Roebuck
& Company
Sears Tower
Chicago, IL 60684

KitchenAid
Division of Hobart
Corporation
Troy, OH 45374

Litton Microwave
Cooking Products
1405 Xenium Lane
Minneapolis, MN 55441

Magic Chef Inc.
740 King Edward Avenue
Cleveland, TN 37311

The Maytag Company
403 West Fourth Street
Newton, IA 50208

Miami-Carey
203 Garver Road
Monroe, OH 45050

Miele Appliances Inc.
12F World's Fair Drive
Sommerset, NJ 08873

Modern Maid Division
McGraw-Edison Company
Box 1111
Chattanooga, TN 37401

Panasonic Company
1 Panasonic Way
Secaucus, NJ 07094

Sub-Zero Freezer
Company, Inc.
Box 4130
Madison, WI 53711

Tappan Company
Tappan Park
Box 606
Mansfield, OH 44901

Thermador/Waste King
Division of Norris Industries
5119 District Boulevard
Los Angeles, CA 90040

Traulson Company
114-02 15th Avenue
College Point, NY 11356

Whirlpool Corporation
Administrative Center
Benton Harbor, MI 49022

White-Westinghouse
Corporation
939 Fort Dusquesne Blvd.
Pittsburgh, PA 15222

ASSOCIATIONS

American Institute of
Architects (AIA)
1735 New York Avenue NW
Washington, DC 20006

National Association of Home Builders (NAHB)
15th and M Streets NW
Washington, DC 20005

National Kitchen and Bath Association
114 Main Street
Hackettstown, NJ 07804

The Tile Council of America
Box 2222
Princeton, NJ 08540

CABINETS

Acorn Manufacturing Company
Box 31
Mansfield, MA 02048

Allmilmo USA
70 Clinton Road
Fairfield, NJ 07006

ALNO-Kitchen Cabinets Inc.
4226 Rivers Avenue
Box 10323
Charleston, SC 29411

Aristokraft Cabinets
Box 420
Jasper, IN 47546

Closet Maid Storage Systems
Clairson International
720 SW 17th Street
Ocala, FL 32674

Eurofit Cabinets
SieMatic USA
7206 Georgetown Road
Santa Barbara, CA 93227

Hafele America Company
Box 1590
High Point, NC 27261

Kitchen Kompact Inc.
KK Plaza
Jeffersonville, IN 47130

Mastercraft Industries Inc.
6175 East 39th Avenue
Denver, CO 80207

Merillat Industries Inc.
2075 West Beecher Road
Adrian, MI 49221

Poggenpohl USA Corporation
6 Pearl Court
Allendale, NJ 07401

QuakerMaid
Division of Tappan
Corporation
Route 61
Leesport, PA 19533

Riviera Kitchens
5401 West Kennedy Blvd.
Tampa, FL 33609

St. Charles Manufacturing Company
1611 East Main Street
St. Charles, IL 60174

Triangle Pacific Corporation
4255 LBJ Freeway
Dallas, TX 75234

FLOORING

Armstrong World Industries
Box 3001
Lancaster, PA 17604

Congoleum Corporation
195 Belgrove Drive
Kearny, NJ 07032

Harris-Tarkett
Resilient Flooring Division
Box 264
Parsippany, NJ 07054

Harris-Tarkett
Wood Flooring Division
Box 300
Johnson City, TN 37605

Kentile Floors Inc.
58 Second Street
Brooklyn, NY 11215

Mannington Mills Inc.
Box 30
Salem, NJ 08079

LAMINATES

DuPont Company
1007 Market Street
Wilmington, DE 19898

Formica Corporation
120 East Fourth Street
Cincinnati, OH 45202

Nevermar Corporation
8339 Telegraph Road
Odenton, MD 21113

Wilsonart
600 General Bruce Drive
Temple, TX 76501

SINKS AND FAUCETS

American Brass Manufacturing Company
500 Superior Avenue
Cleveland, OH 44103

American Standard Inc.
Box 2003
New Brunswick, NJ 08903

Arundale Inc.
1173 Reco Avenue
St. Louis, MO 63126

Chicago Faucet Company
2100 South Nuclear Drive
Des Plaines, IL 60018

Crane Plumbing Division
300 Park Avenue
New York, NY 10022

Delta Faucet Company
Box 40980
55 East 111th Street
Indianapolis, IN 46280

Eljer Plumbingware
Wallace Murray Corporation
Three Gateway Center
Pittsburgh, PA 15222

Elkay Manufacturing Company
2222 Camden Court
Oak Brook, IL 60521

Grohe America Inc.
900 Lively Boulevard
Wood Dale, IL 60191

Indiana Brass Inc.
Box 369
Frankfort, IN 46041

Kohler Company
High Street
Kohler, WI 53044

Milwaukee Faucets Inc.
4250 North 124th Street
Milwaukee, WI 53222

Moen Division of Standyne
377 Woodland Avenue
Elyria, OH 44036

The Revere Sink Corporation
44 Coffin Avenue
New Bedford, MA 02746

Stainless Steel Sink Inc.
300 Fay Avenue
Box 296
Adison, IL 60101

TILE

American Olean Tile Company
1000 Cannon Avenue
Landsdale, PA 19446

Gilmer Potteries Inc.
Box 489
Gilmer, TX 75644

Hasting Tile Company
201 East 57th Street
New York, NY 10022

Hunting-Pacific Ceramics Inc
Box 1149
Corona, CA 91718

Italian Tile Center
499 Park Avenue
New York, NY 10022

Summitville Tiles Inc.
Box 73
Summitville, OH 43962

Wenczel Tile Company
Box 5308
Trenton, NJ 08638

Windburn Tile Manufacturing Company
Box 1369
Little Rock, AK 72203

WINDOWS AND BLINDS

Andersen Corporation
Bayport, MN 55003

Caradco Corporation
Box 920
Rantoul, IL 61866

Hurd Millwork Company
520 South Whelen Avenue
Medford, WI 54451

Levolor Lorentzen Inc.
1 Upper Pond Road
Parsippany, NJ 07054

Marvin Windows
Box 100 Highway 11
Warroad, MN 56763

Pella/Rolscreen Company
100 Main Street
Pella, IA 50219

Velux-America Inc.
Box 3268
Greenwood, SC 29648

Webb Manufacturing Inc.
Box 707
Conneaut, OH 44030

Index